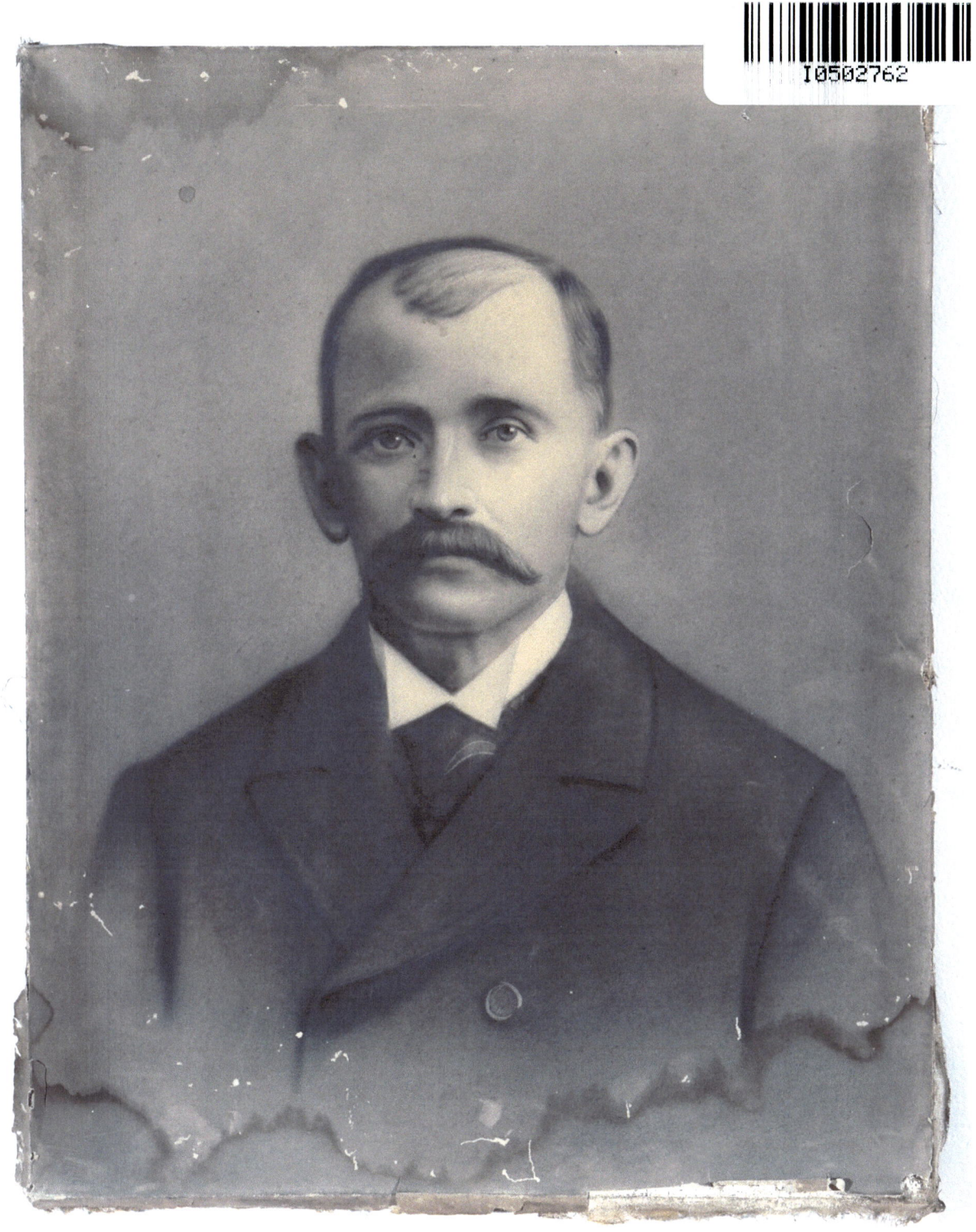

Hamilton Stillwell, 1916
Photographer Unknown

The Hamilton Stillwell Collection
1916-1918

Adam Blue

Stone House Press
247 Burr Road
Cornish, NH 03745

Special thanks to Charley Freiberg
charleyfreibergphotography.com

First Printing, 2015

ISBN: 1505393345
ISBN-13: 978-1505393347

This book is lovingly dedicated
to my family.

When we moved to a Cornish, NH farmhouse in the summer of 2006, we were excited by the possibilities that lay ahead. Once our boxes were unpacked, I started searching the nearby woods for creative inspiration. Hidden in a hemlock grove just beyond the property line, I discovered an abandoned cabin. I approached via the side deck and peeked in the blackened windows. Little was revealed. Drawn next to the back door, I strode down the porch. My boot broke through a rotten plank and I fell to the ground. My ears rang as I picked myself up and started looking for an alternative entry. Luckily, the memory of my daughter's laugh returned me to my senses. I rubbed my neck and backed away slowly, heading home in the dusk light.

Unable to shake my instinct for the site, I ventured back two weeks later. Months had passed since I had last used my paints or camera. Writing felt a chore. There was something for me in that cabin, I was certain. Some kind of breakthrough, I could feel it in my gut. With a dull machete in one hand and a depleted Bic lighter in the other, I forced the door. In a million years, I never would have anticipated what I found inside: an unknown cache of artworks by Hamilton Stillwell, one of the region's most prescient artists of the early 20th century.

Between 1916 and 1918, Hamilton Stillwell was an essential member of the Cornish Colony. But he is conspicuously absent from the substantial documentation detailing this period. Why? I kept asking myself as I compulsively looked into his life. Was he innocently forgotten by time? Was he expunged from the record deliberately? For every problem my research solved, two new questions arose. Soon, my every stray thought went spinning down this rabbit hole, and my faith in the tenets of history was challenged. How is it possible to erase an artist's life? Was this whole experience some kind of farce? *Would I never know—would I never know!?*

Taken on its own terms, Stillwell's work clearly deserved recognition. But like any echo of the past, he may have been more mirror than man—a remnant onto which I layered myself, knowing he was safely eclipsed by time. As the complexities of his tale compounded, and as I invested more of my life into this search for significance, the rewards for my efforts redoubled. Though it was a struggle to produce, it is a pleasure to share what I found.

A world traveler, logician, and bootlegger, Hamilton Stillwell contributed a river of fine, hand-crafted spirits to the Upper Valley's social festivities at the turn of the 20th century. This popular feat alone should have won him a place in the local canon. But it did not. Some testimonials I heard suggested that his incendiary temper, enflamed by the product he distributed, was responsible for his erasure from local history. Others argued it was his immigrant status, his deficiency of blue blood and lack of birthright that kept him from finding success in this stubborn town. Then again, it also could have been his vigorous insistence that abstract artistic forms were a more modern mode of visual representation than the post-impressionist and neo-classical aesthetics that dominated the area. Somewhere in this mix lay the reason for Stillwell's omission from our regional narrative.

❧

Hamilton Stillwell was born to modest means in Montreal, Quebec in 1890. His father, second-generation British from Colebrook, NH, was a baker who immigrated to the urban environs of Canada. Before and after school, young Stillwell helped with the family business, becoming fluent in the craft of baking as well as French and English. He produced loaf after sculptural loaf during this time, and his innovative designs garnered culinary fame for his family. In particular, one oversized gingerbread house, strikingly similar to what would later be recognized as a Le Corbusier tenement, won the premier award at the 1903 Jean Talon Market Winter Pavilion celebrations. Unfortunately, none of his earliest works can be found in this volume, since they were eaten within days of their creation.

When he turned eighteen, Stillwell sought his fortune on the continent of Europe. He signed onto *Le Concord*, a pointy-nosed vessel that marked its trans-Atlantic departures with a "boom" of cannon fire, a peculiar feat for an unarmed merchant ship.

After a period of unaccounted for vagrancy in the French countryside, Stillwell secured work at *Fondations*, a Parisian patisserie. The owner, Marcel Contreneau, was an artisan of the highest order and was firmly committed to the proletarian lifestyle. Though the Arrondissement's elites regularly patronized his bakery, Contreneau reserved his finest creations for fellow tradesmen, artists, and musicians. Because he believed so strongly in the importance of cultural production, he had his apprentice deliver fresh bread to artists' studios each day at noon. On his route, young Stillwell befriended visionaries like Picasso, Braque, Hoch, Delaney, Matisse, and Picabia. The impressionable youth absorbed more from them than he understood: their lines, planes, arcs, and colors became part of his consciousness. And he learned to take pleasure in supporting their work, as his daily visits fortified their bodies while keeping their hands and minds engaged with their higher purpose.

Though never spoken of publicly, it was no secret that Marcel Contreneau was a hedonist who found other uses for the yeast he had in his bakery. It was rumored that he produced the finest beers and distilled liquors in the district. It was known that he held the finest parties. His assistant figured prominently in the scene. By twenty-two years of age, Stillwell had grown into a champion of fiery late-night talk, of casual dances turned sensuous, of bravado displays of will.

In 1915, Stillwell's sister fell ill, and he was called back to Montreal. Though he dreaded his return to North America and the responsibilities that lay ahead, the journey changed him in unexpected ways. On his second Atlantic crossing, he shared a cabin with Henri d'Agnon, a philosopher and master logician from Nice. Their conversations ranged from the trivial to the sublime. By the end of the voyage, all of Stillwell's perspectives were informed by a new system of understanding. He was now able to interpret the world through patterns, through relationships defined by vectors, durations, and volumes. Stillwell's early intuitive successes with geometries in dough now had a rising vocabulary. His creative purpose became clear, and the conceptual keys to his production were firmly in his grasp.

Days after being reunited with his family, Stillwell's sister died. Unusual circumstances complicated her passing. After Stillwell's first private audience with her body, the mortician's son, a voyeur and aspiring street photographer, captured an image of her corpse set among a lattice of transecting lines and pastel-painted planes. The boy sold his surreptitious photograph to the local press, and the rumor mill confused Stillwell's progressive spiritual rites with perverse, satanic ritual. Uncertain if religious or municipal authorities were looking to press charges, Stillwell left Quebec under cloak of darkness. Though his faith in his analytical methods was unshaken, his trust in others diminished.

He sought amnesty in the United States, venturing to the rugged landscape of northern New Hampshire and his father's roots. Upon arriving in Colebrook,

Stillwell heard word of the Cornish Colony. Drawn as he was to creative and artistic perspectives, he assumed he would find an environment like the one he knew in Paris. In a flash of inspiration, he departed south, never having unpacked his bags.

Stillwell established his Cornish studio in the summer of 1916. Following the model he'd learned in France, he mingled among the upper-class artists, but lived within the community of farmers, shepherds, and tradesmen. His radical perspectives on abstract art and continental philosophy alienated the neo-classical colonists; his absent birthright diminished him in the eyes of the native born. Neither group took him into their fold, but all welcomed his Parisian tinctures. So he was received, to a degree, wherever he wandered.

Curiously, Stillwell felt most welcome at quilting bees, where the women's sensible geometries were strong and clear. He appreciated how the quilts told stories, too—each its own abstract representation of a moment in someone's life. His preference for quilting, and the company of quilters, was of purely aesthetic intention, though likely informed in part by his incomplete mourning over his sister's death. Unfortunately, the local male leadership, for whom quilting served to generate a bonus allotment of time for their own unsupervised revelries, grew increasingly paranoid about his involvement with their wives and daughters, further marginalizing Stillwell from those individuals endowed with crafting history.

Always determined to advance his own art, Stillwell exhausted himself explaining the relevance of his creative vision. He expounded at length upon how he'd woven life's complex milestones into his work—births and deaths, exultations and tragedies—and how he aspired to represent all social forces and formative experiences in his geometries. His neighbors nodded intently as they accepted his refreshments, but invariably had a change of heart when their cups were dry and it was time to support his vision. Stillwell's estimation of others sank lower. But he did not despair as his relationships waned. He altered his mission.

In a drunken epiphany over Thanksgiving weekend in 1918, Stillwell realized that the perfect audience for his work was American corporations, their executives, and the institutions of art they influenced. He had previously avoided the business world whenever possible, as its champions' success came through maximizing every margin for their exclusive benefit. Stillwell's analytic philosophy revealed that in practice, not only did their system require inequity to thrive, it perversely rewarded exploiting the relative weakness of others. He revisited his glass of brandy and gazed at the glowing embers in his fire. Perhaps he, and his art, would play by their rules now, too. It would be neither fun, nor difficult. He sighed. Why not meet them on their terms, distasteful as they may be? His experience had shown that making art for individuals was fruitless from a business perspective, as most of the people he spoke with wanted to buy newer versions of older ideas whose validity had already been popularized, and arguably, diluted. Making art for the government was completely out of the question, since politicians prospered by embodying the worst facets of the people he no longer wanted to court. But corporations, and especially the well-funded executives who had internalized their company's moral code—his abstractions would suit their needs perfectly! By displaying his geometries, businessmen could demonstrate their commitment to culture without alienating their customers or colleagues with imagery that could offend. And, by holding his work in their prestigious collections, they could add value to their initial investment, staging future profits when the time came to flip his work at auction. He gulped down more of his blueberry spirits. One day soon, he thought, exchange value will be the only arbiter of aesthetic quality in western culture. For art to exist at all in the future, a solid return on investment will eclipse the hope of communicating human experience by virtue of necessity.

In a rapid reversal of fortune, Stillwell rubbed his eyes and understood that even though his symbolic abstractions felt burdensome in 1918, the opaque language he employed was his work's greatest asset. All beauty, all compassion, all content be damned. He shook his head as a wet dog might. One hundred years hence, discourse will be double-speak and the truth will take refuge in satire. He drained the last of his bottle and cast it across the room. With singular resolve, Stillwell pushed back his chair and threw his studio notes into the fire—burning away the spiritual core of his visual language in order to save it—and redacted the titles from every work in his studio.

❧

With hindsight, Hamilton Stillwell's artistic production between the years 1916 and 1918 was a fusion of his early influences: the time he spent with his hands in dough; the continental sensibilities he sampled in France; his emergent philosophy of life's gestures notated through abstract form and color; his access to tradesmen's tools and domestic textiles as source materials; and finally, his decision to pervert his vision for a society serving corporations. Each facet of his work was revolutionary in its own right, with many touchstones remaining outside the popular sphere of American art for decades. Stillwell undoubtedly suffered for his art between 1916 and 1918, yet these years were essential to his creative development.

In early December 1918, Stillwell aggressively tried to settle his accounts with the merry-making artists who had long dodged payment for his drinks. This final act, when combined with his persistent and unusual ideas about art and the abundant social time he spent sewing with the region's women, caused the men to turn on him en masse. His tactless debt-collecting strategies proved the last straw, and once again, Stillwell needed a new home.

Then one night, he was gone. Some people assumed he returned to Paris, others suggested he'd departed towards the commercial interests in Boston. A rumor circulated that he had been spotted at an art opening in Peterborough, NH, but no one knew if it was true. He had vanished from Cornish as abruptly as he had arrived.

Undoubtedly, Hamilton Stillwell's presence in the Upper Valley violated the normative structure of the region's art community at the turn of the 20th century. Once absent, our civic leaders decided, through both passive and active means, that his name would not be uttered, and that his work would not be shown. With this simple gesture, his tale was swept beneath the rug and his omission was confirmed as reality.

History can be fickle in this way. Sometimes it's right. Sometimes it's wrong. Often, it reveals the author with greater accuracy than it portrays the past. Nevertheless, history will always be a story. And like any good one, it reads best when it touches upon the truth, even though it's fiction.

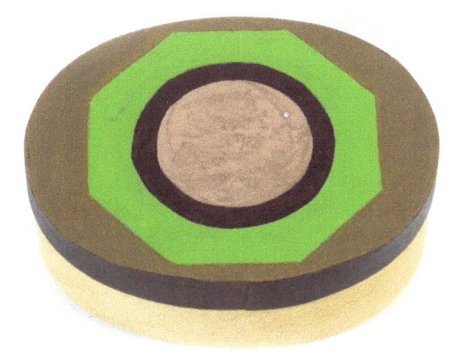

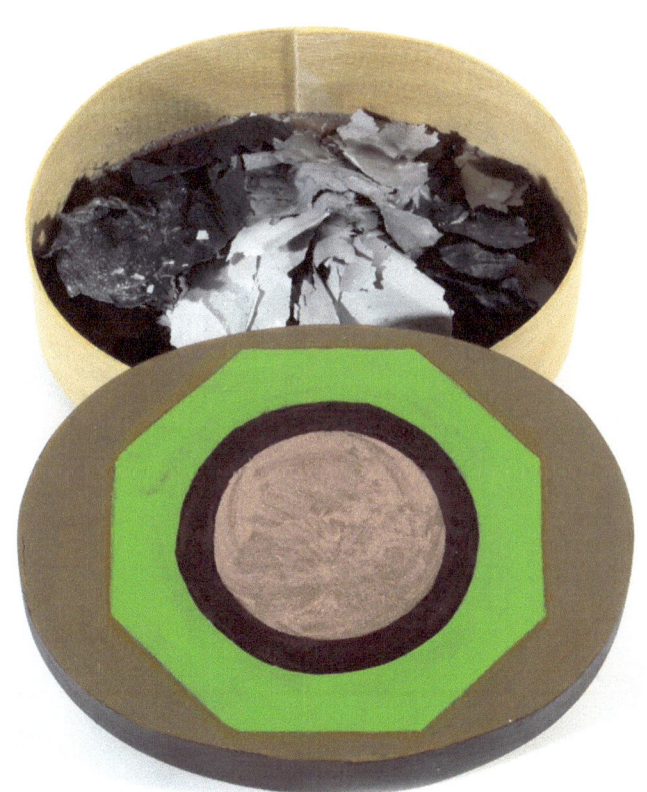

~~Phoenix~~
6" x 4½" x 2"
Wood, Ash, Oil Paint

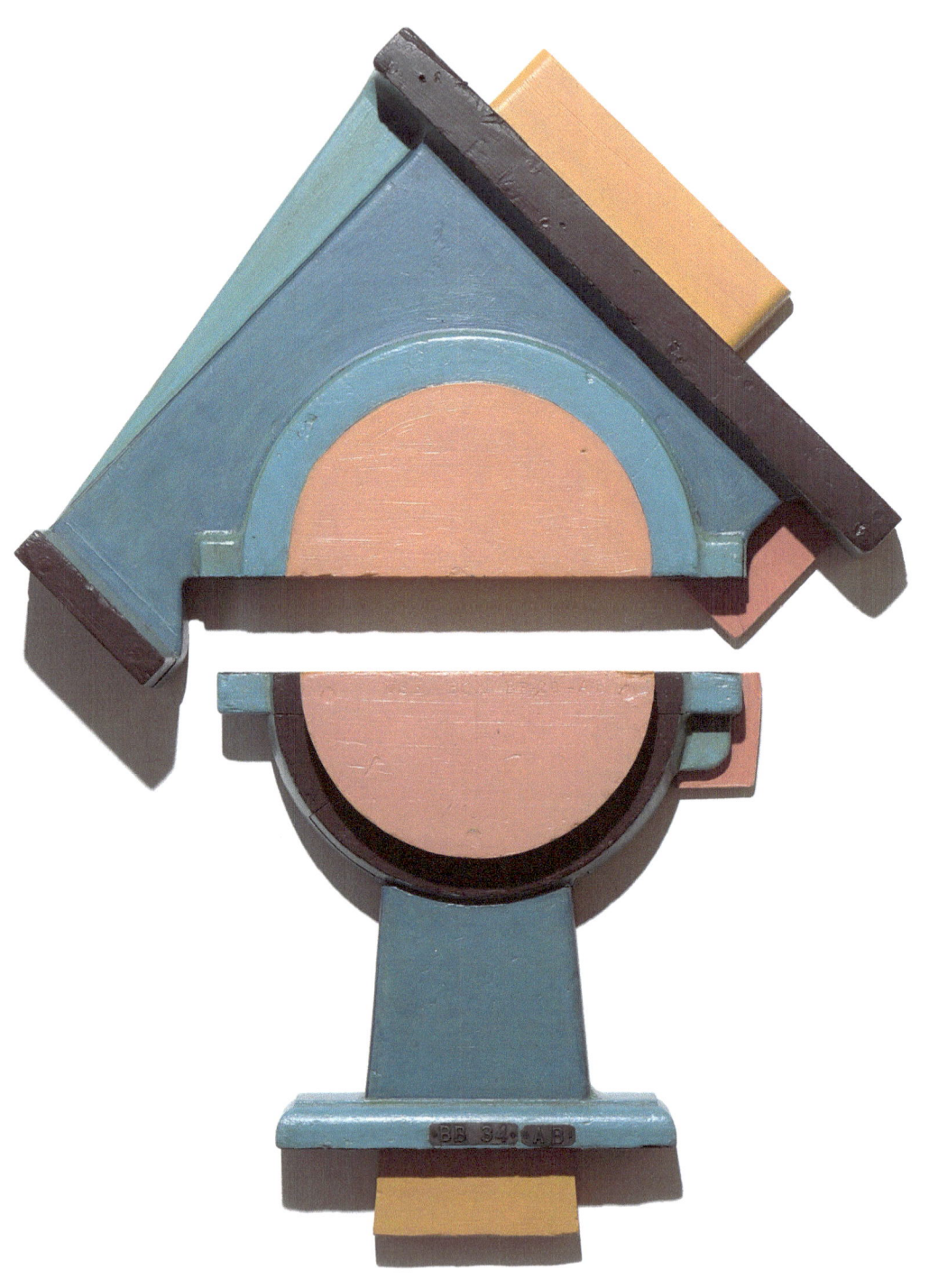

Angelica Stillwell
19½" x 36" x 4"
Wood, Tin, Oil Paint

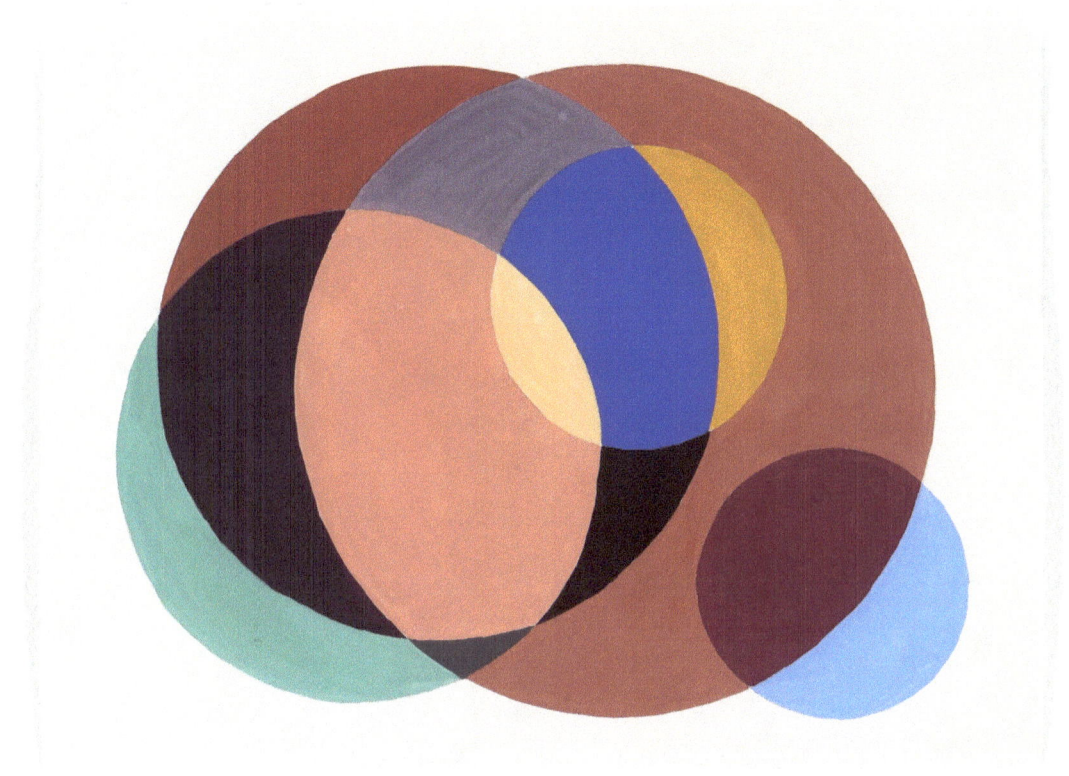

Imperialism and the Great War
12" x 9"
Gouache on Paper

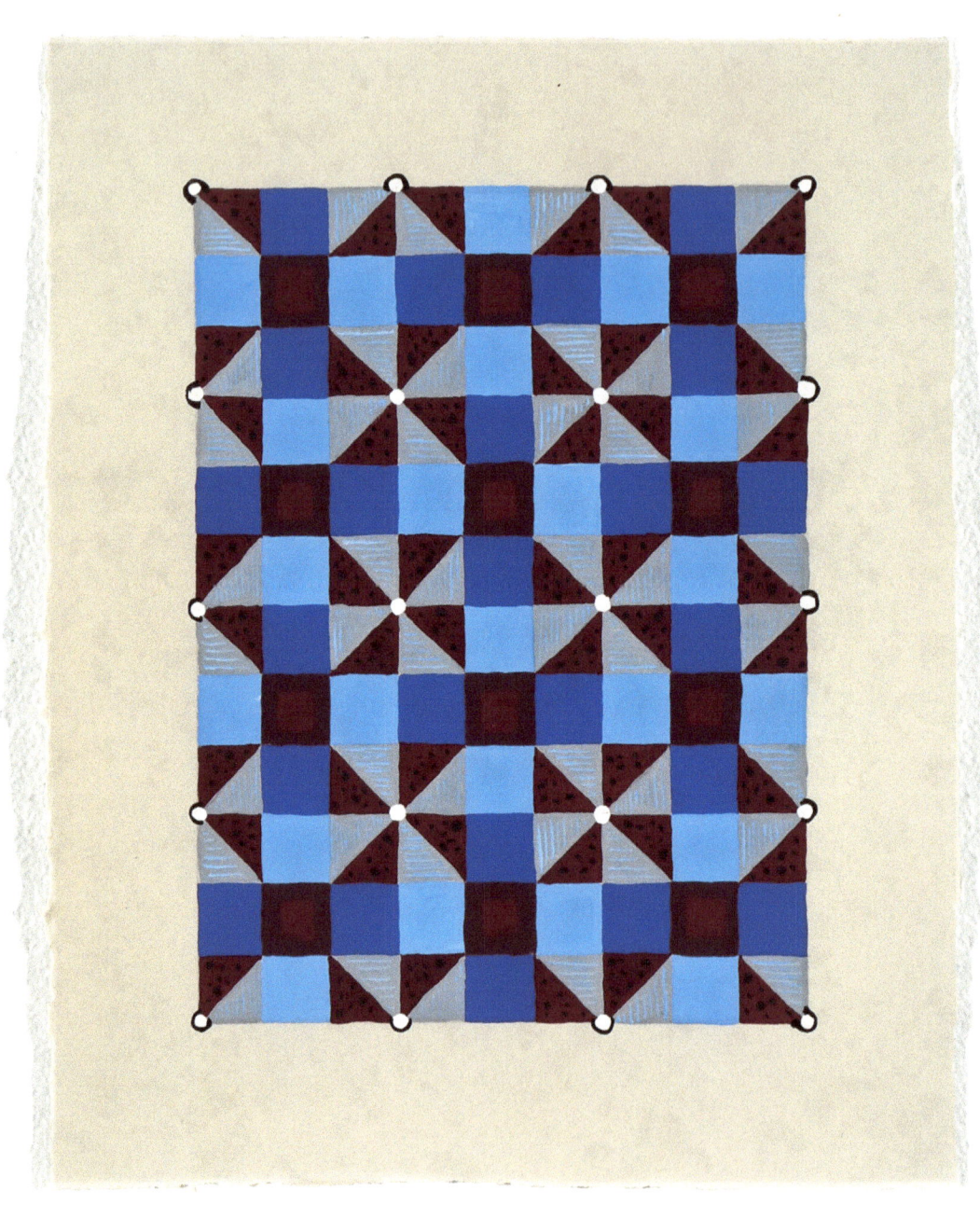

Great Art Comforts the Disturbed
and Disturbs the Comfortable
9¾" x 12"
Gouache on Paper

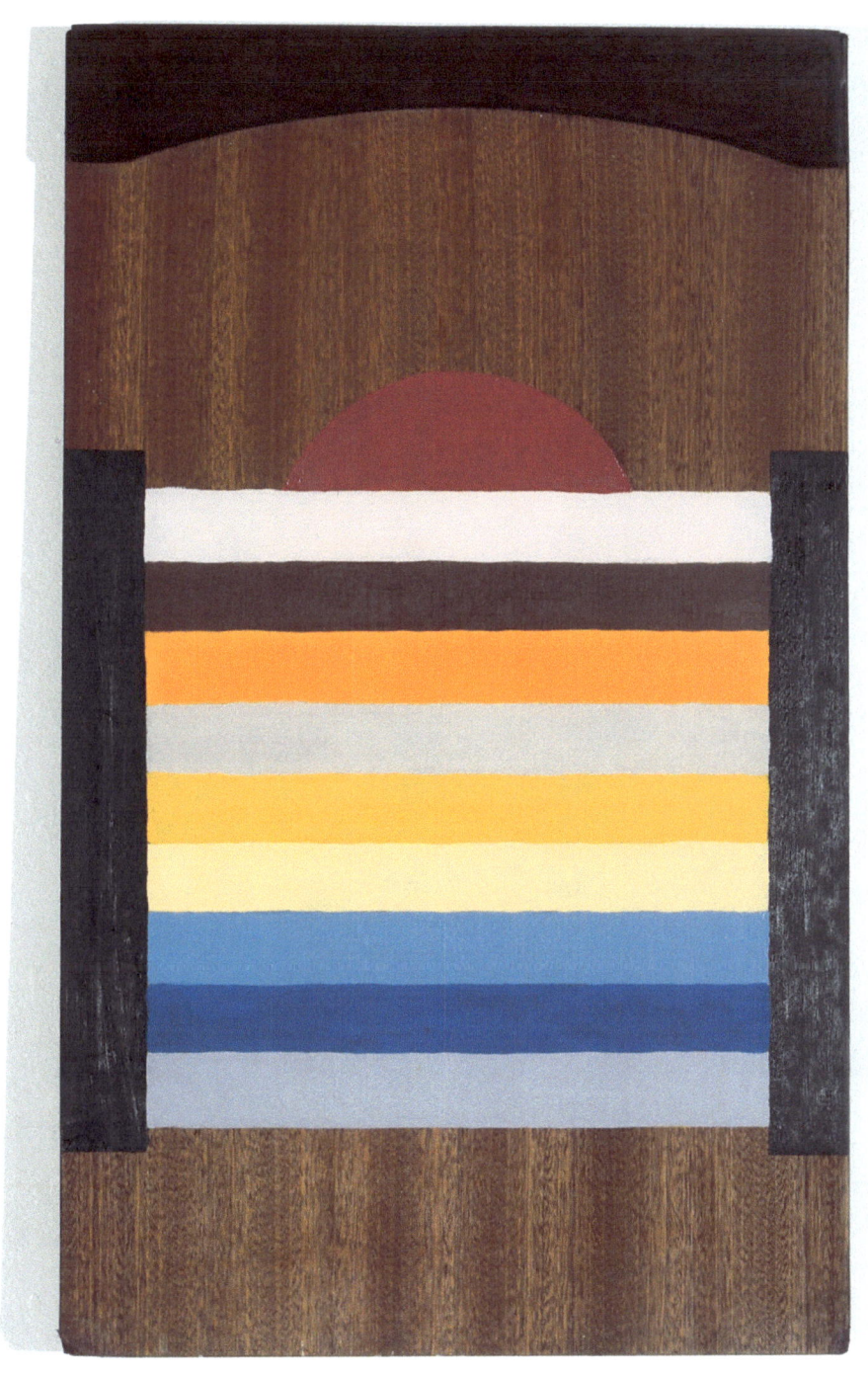

Forget the Train, Freedom Is a Driver's License
14" x 23" x 1½"
Wood, Oil Paint

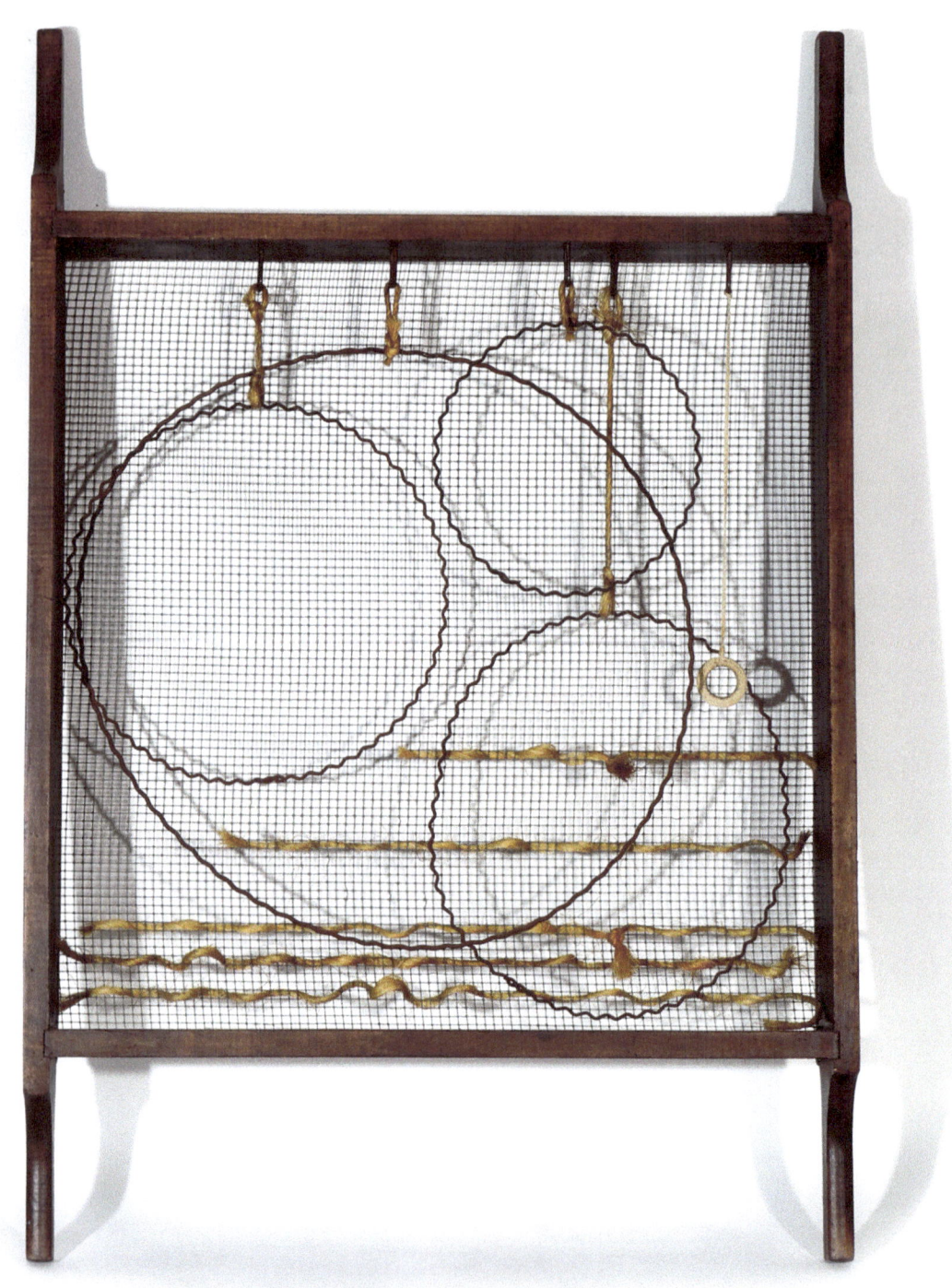

All Revolutionary Instincts Are Constrained
by the Fabric of Society
24" x 36" x 4½"
Wood, Wire Mesh, Barrel Rings, Twine, Window Shade Pull

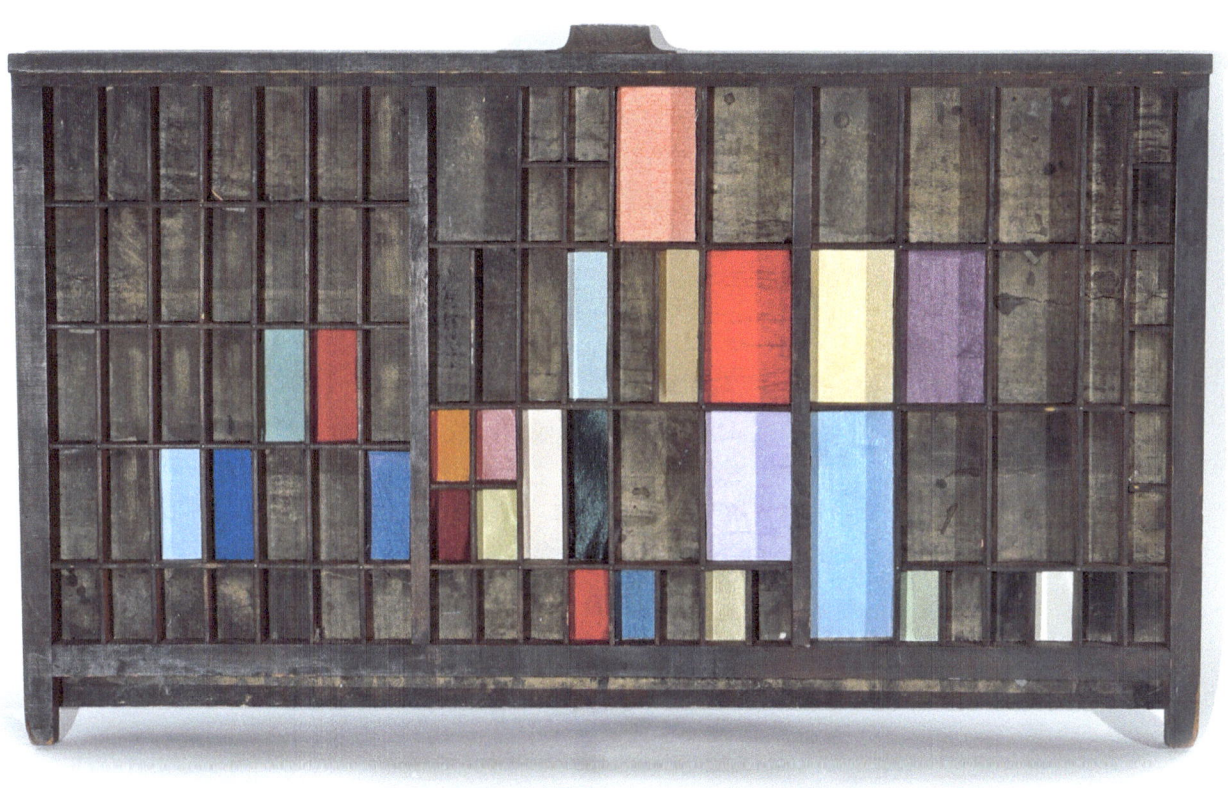

~~Dancing in 4/4~~
32½" x 18" x 2"
Wood, Metal, Quilting Scraps

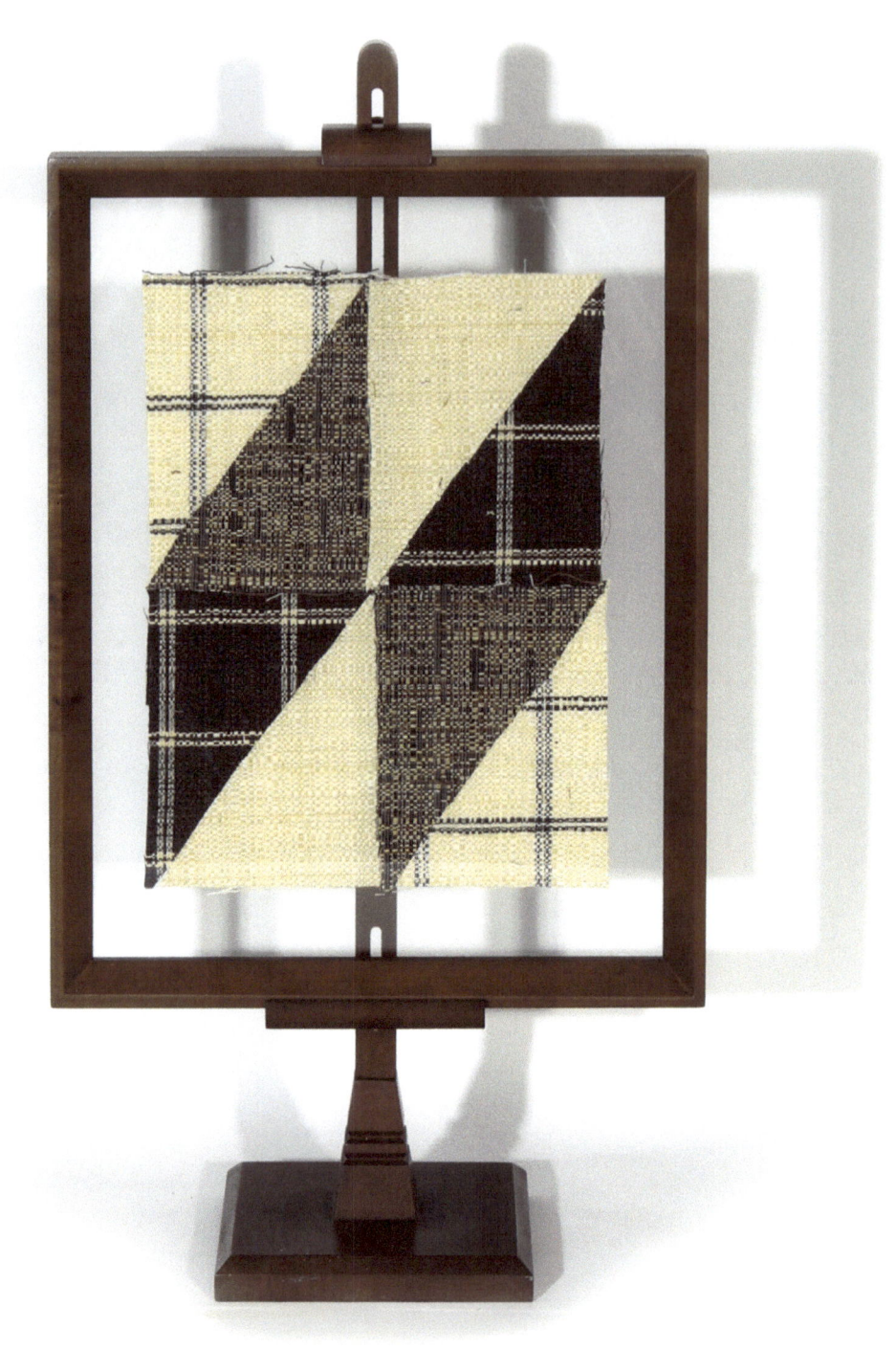

~~Zombie Formalism:~~
~~A Perfect Fit for the Marketplace~~
12" x 22" x 6"
Wood, Glass, Quilting Scraps

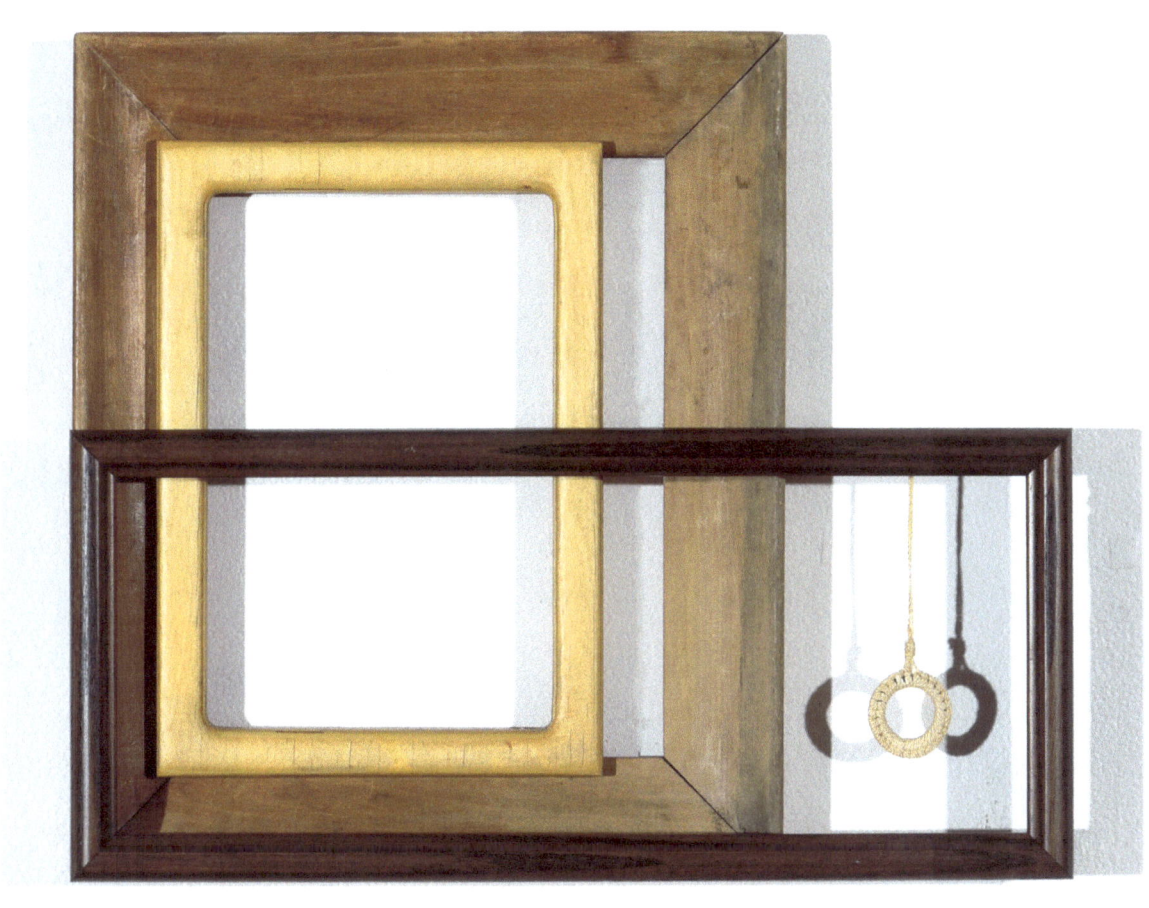

A Society of Individuals Serving Themselves
Isn't a Society at All
16" x 13½" x 2"
Wood, Window Shade Pull

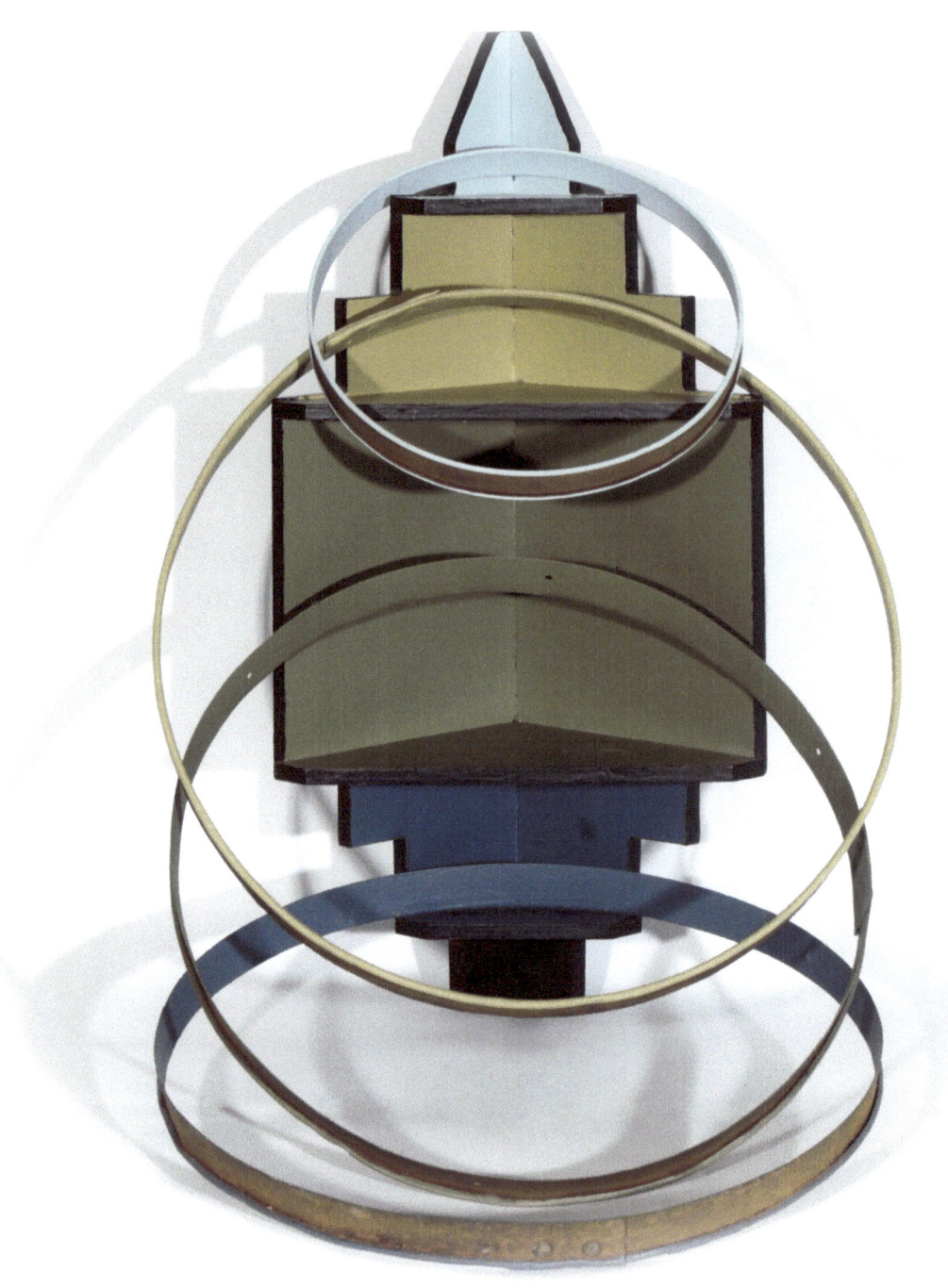

Perhaps a Hug Would Help
16" x 24½" x 18"
Wood, Barrel Rings, Oil Paint

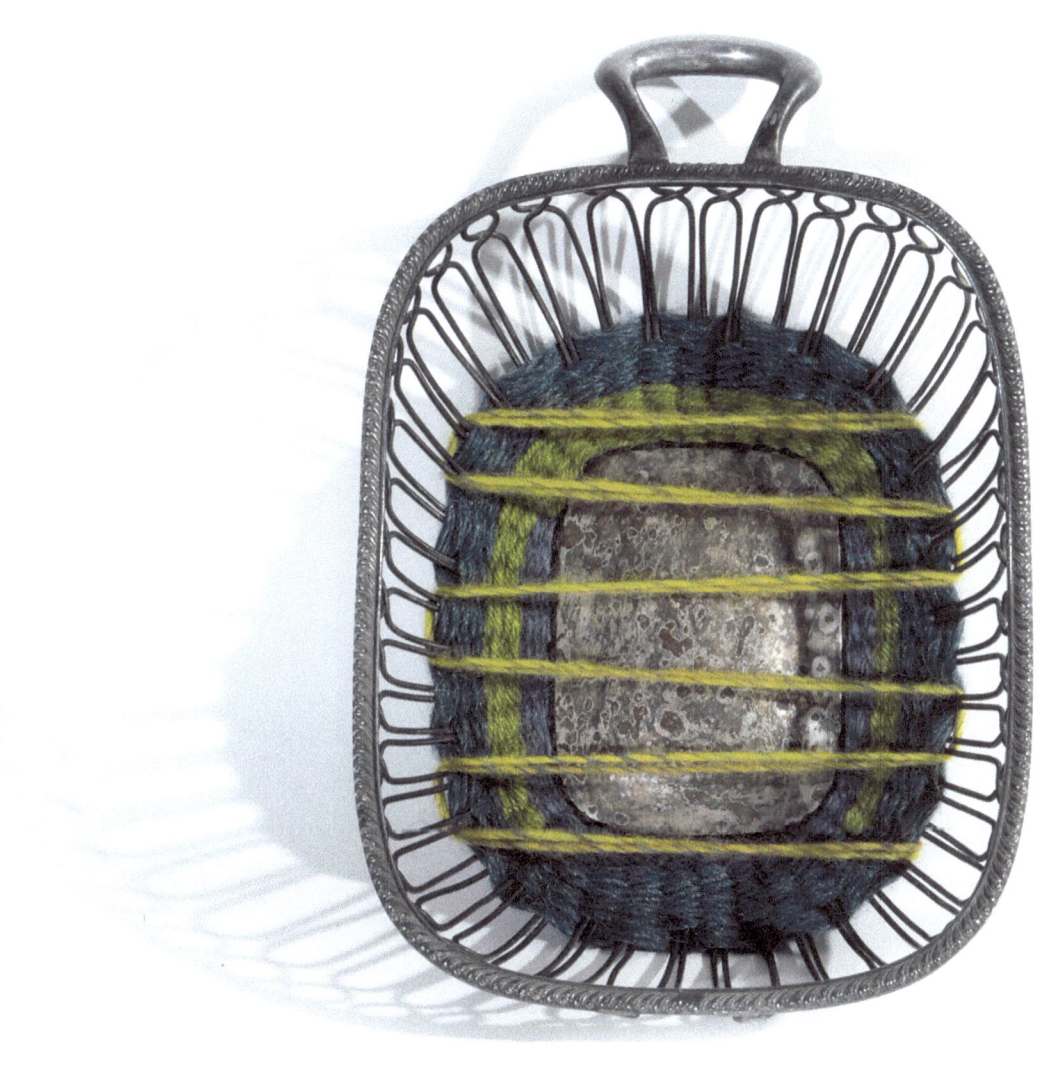

In Every Moment, The Infinite
7" x 10" x 3½"
Sterling Silver Basket, Yarn

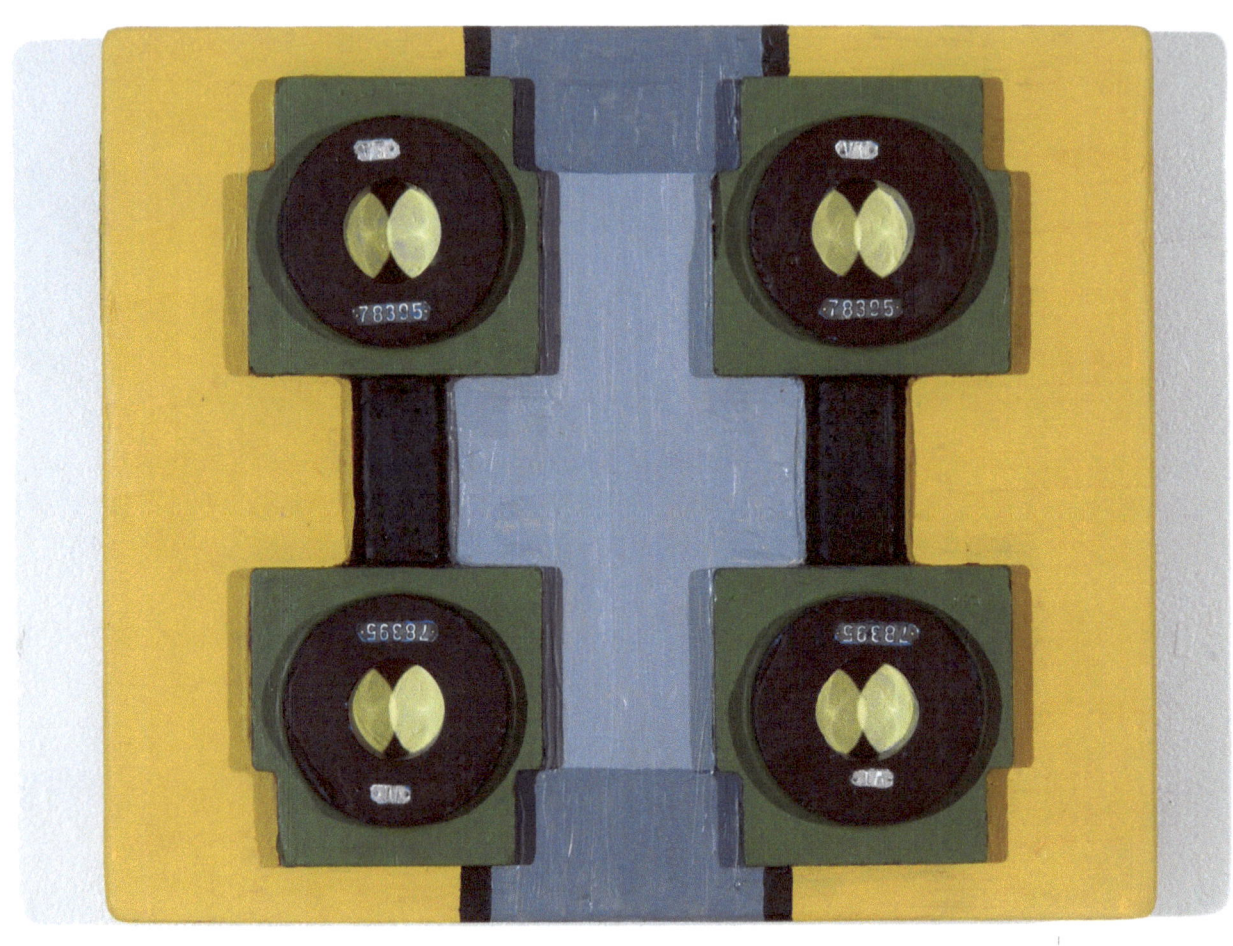

Worker, Brother
Artist, Lover
16" x 14" x 2½"
Wood, Tin, Oil Paint

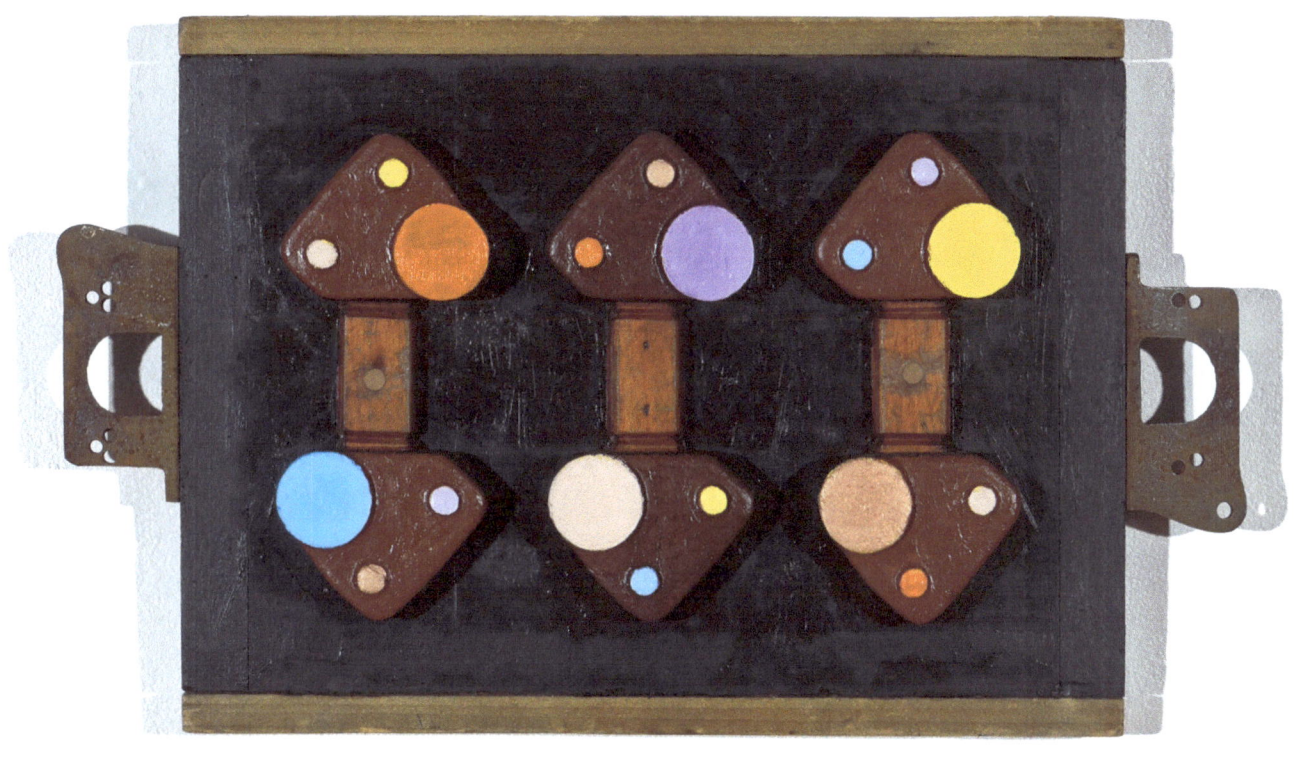

Cultures Are Discrete, Concrete, and Arbitrary
22½" x 13½" x 3"
Wood, Steel, Oil Paint

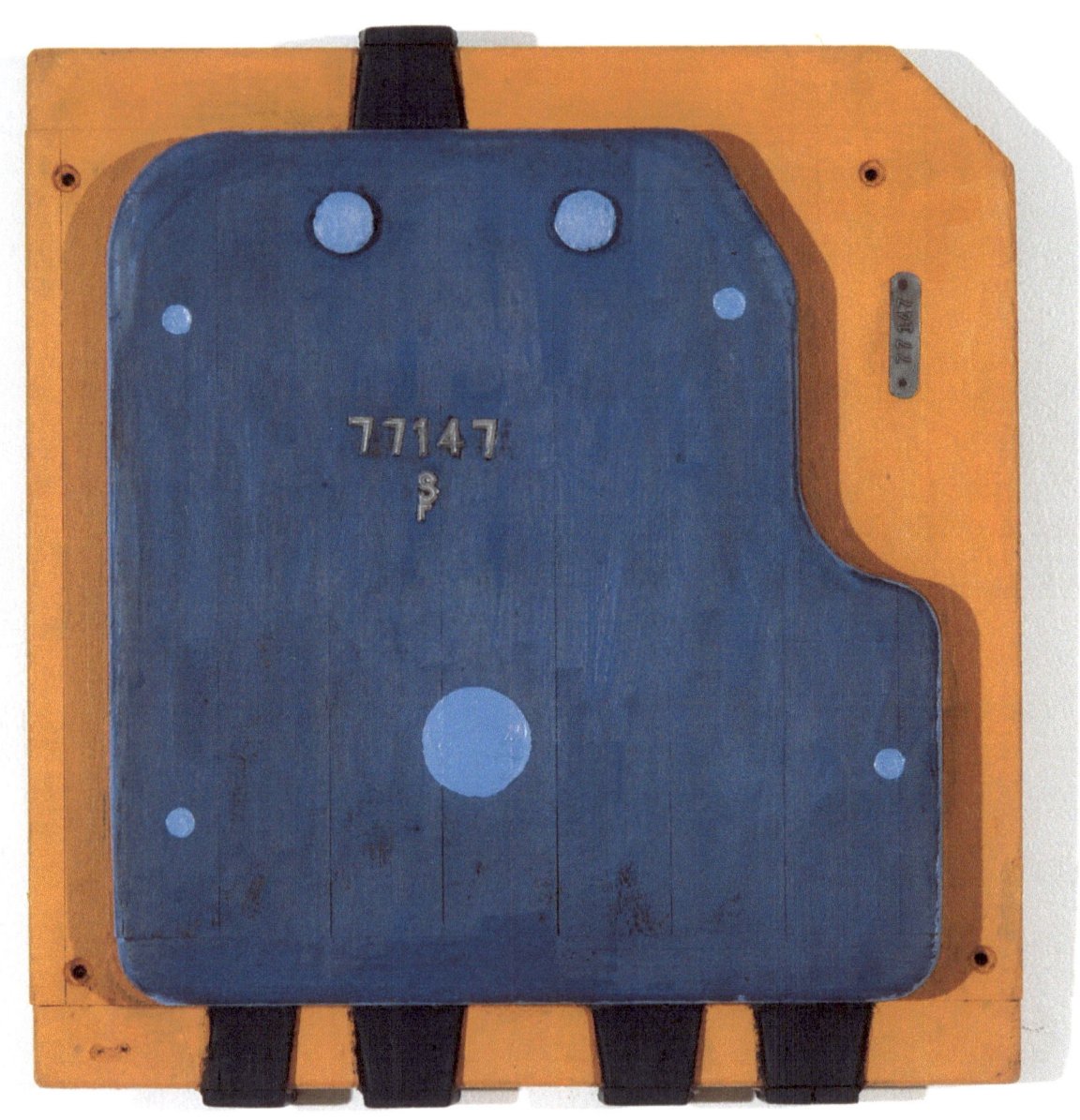

When I Say "Don't", You Say "Stop"
"Don't" "_____", "Don't" "_____"
13" x 17" x 3"
Wood, Tin, Oil Paint

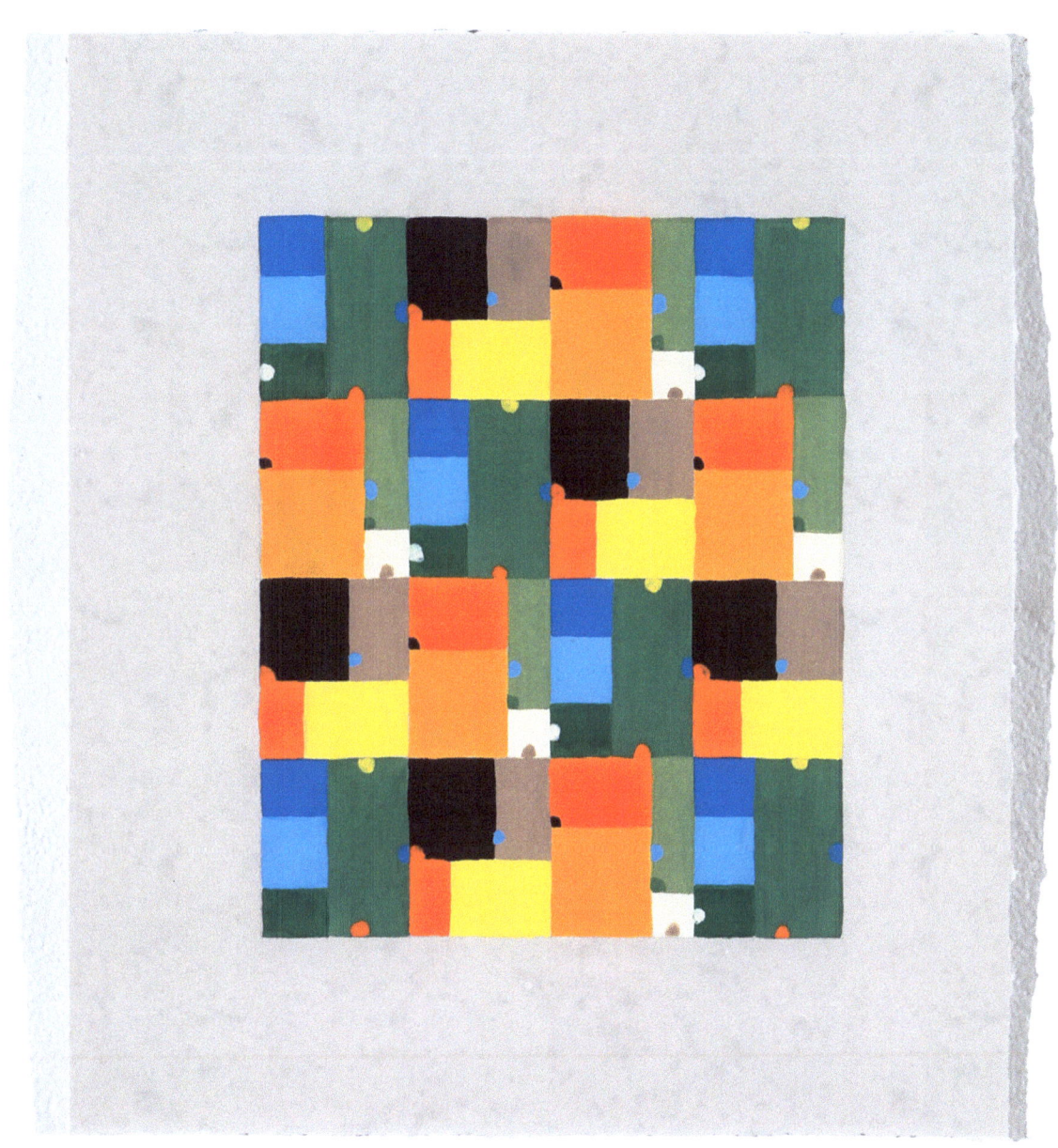

~~Let Them Eat Kale~~
9" x 11"
Gouache on Paper